PANDAS

by Jennifer Zeiger

Children's Press®

An Imprint of Scholastic Inc.
New York   Toronto   London   Auckland   Sydney
Mexico City   New Delhi   Hong Kong
Danbury, Connecticut

Content Consultant
Dr. Stephen S. Ditchkoff
Professor of Wildlife Sciences
Auburn University
Auburn, Alabama

Photographs © 2012: age fotostock: 35 (Dave Stamboulis), 23,
39 (Eric Baccega), 27 (Michele Wassell), 8 (Shigeki Tanaka);
Alamy Images: 31 (C. Huetter/Arco Images GmbH), 7 (Steve
Bloom Images); AP Images: 5 bottom, 36 (Charles Dharapak),
28 (Hedalu), 32 (Max Vision); Bob Italiano: 44 foreground, 45
foreground; Dreamstime: cover (Goodolga), 2 background, 3
background (Lidian Neeleman), 5 background, 44 background, 45
background (Rewat Wannasuk); Minden Pictures/Katherine Feng: 20;
National Geographic/Katherine Feng/Globio/Minden Pictures: 15;
Shutterstock, Inc.: 4, 12 (hironai), 11 (Hung Chung Chih); Superstock:
5 top, 19 (age fotostock), 16, 24 (Minden Pictures); The Image
Works/Peters/ullstein bild: 1, 3 foreground, 40.

Library of Congress Cataloging-in-Publication Data
  Pandas/by Jennifer Zeiger.
    p. cm.—(Nature's children)
  Includes bibliographical references and index.
  ISBN-13: 978-0-531-20905-9 (lib. bdg.)
    ISBN-10: 0-531-20905-9 (lib. bdg.)
  ISBN-13: 978-0-531-21080-2 (pbk.)
    ISBN-10: 0-531-21080-4 (pbk.)
  1. Pandas—Juvenile literature. I. Title. II. Series.
  QL737.C27Z435 2012
  599.789—dc23   2011031076

All rights reserved. Published in 2012 by Children's Press, an imprint
of Scholastic Inc.
Printed in China 62
SCHOLASTIC, CHILDREN'S PRESS, and associated logos are
trademarks and/or registered trademarks of Scholastic Inc.

1 2 3 4 5 6 7 8 9 10 R 21 20 19 18 17 16 15 14 13 12

Pandas

Class	Mammalia
Order	Carnivora
Family	Ursidae
Genus	*Ailuropoda*
Species	*Ailuropoda melanoleuca*
World distribution	Central China, near the Tibetan Plateau
Habitat	Cold, humid bamboo forests in mountainous areas
Distinctive physical characteristics	Bearlike appearance; black-and-white fur; a round, white face with full cheeks and black markings around the eyes and ears
Habits	Mostly live alone; rub themselves on rocks and trees to leave scent; young pandas can climb trees to escape danger; adults roar to scare off attackers
Diet	Mainly eats the leaves, shoots, and stems of bamboo; occasionally eats meat if it is easily available

Contents

CHAPTER 1

The Popular Panda

Pandas are popular. In zoos around the world, pandas always draw huge crowds. Zoo visitors all want to see a panda chomping on a tough piece of bamboo or snoring in the corner. Sometimes a panda's furry black-and-white face appears to be smiling or laughing. These bears seem friendly in captivity.

But pandas are very shy. They are hard to find in the wild. They usually live alone. They avoid each other as much as they avoid people. Their home high in the mountains of central China can make them difficult to reach. There are only a few thousand left in the world. Even scientists who study pandas have difficulty tracking them down.

Pandas are always one of the most-visited animals in zoos.

A Different Kind of Bear

All pandas have similar markings. Their bodies are mostly white. Their legs, ears, nose, and the areas around their eyes are black. This type of coloring is not common in other bears. Most bears are one color, usually brown or black. Pandas are also small compared to many other bears. A male panda can grow to be around 250 pounds (113 kilograms). Females are a little smaller. They weigh closer to 220 pounds (100 kg) or less. In comparison, a polar bear can weigh more than 1,000 pounds (454 kg). This is more than four times larger than a panda!

But pandas do share many traits with other bears. They have four legs and are covered in fur. They can stand upright on their back legs if they need to. Pandas can also run on all four legs. But they prefer to sit or lie in the shade.

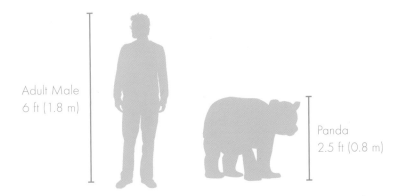

Adult Male
6 ft (1.8 m)

Panda
2.5 ft (0.8 m)

Pandas are much taller when they stand on their back legs.

Shy Creatures

Pandas tend to be shy animals. They live alone in small **home ranges**. Pandas usually live at **altitudes** of around 5,000 to 10,000 feet (1,524 to 3,048 meters) above sea level. This is high in the mountains where the air is cool and wet. Bamboo is everywhere. Some pandas move to a higher altitude during the summer. Temperatures there stay slightly cooler. They travel back down to their winter homes when the seasons change.

Pandas' home ranges often overlap. Parts are shared with other pandas. But the pandas rarely meet each other. They instead communicate through scent. Pandas rub their rumps and urinate on trees, rocks, or other objects. This leaves a scent that tells other pandas about the panda that left it. A panda can learn another panda's gender and social status from this scent.

Pandas spend most of their time alone.

CHAPTER 2

Panda Survival

Pandas are herbivores. This means that they mostly eat plants. Pandas are especially adapted to eat bamboo. Bamboo is a kind of grass that grows in many different climates. More than 1,000 species of bamboo are common to the mountains where pandas live. Bamboo is tough and woody. It grows in tall, hard stalks. Pandas use their claws to slice bamboo stalks. Their sharp front teeth help them bite pieces from the stalk. Wide, flat teeth called molars help them chew the pieces.

This is where a panda's pudgy cheeks come in handy. These cheeks can make the panda look childlike and cuddly. But these friendly-looking cheeks hide muscular jaws. Pandas use their powerful jaws to bite and chew through thick bamboo stalks.

Pandas spend a lot of time eating.

An Unlikely Herbivore

A panda has a digit that it can use as a thumb. It is actually an extra-large wrist bone. But it can move independently of the other **digits**. This allows the panda to hold the bamboo as it eats.

Panda stomachs cannot digest many parts of the bamboo. The bears solve this problem by eating a lot of it. A panda eats about 20 to 40 pounds (9 to 18 kg) of bamboo each day. This supplies their bodies with lots of the nutrients their stomachs can process. The rest leaves their bodies as waste.

FUN FACT! Pandas spend two-thirds of their lives eating. That's 16 hours a day!

Few animals are able to grab things the way pandas can.

Keeping Warm

The weather is cold and humid where pandas live. The air is always moist from rain or the mist that hangs over the forests. Pandas must keep warm and dry to survive in this environment.

A panda is covered in thick fur. This keeps its body's natural heat in. The fur is covered in a little bit of oil. The oil keeps moisture away from the panda's skin. The panda would get cold quickly if its skin became moist. Temperatures are never very warm where pandas live, so pandas keep their coats all year long. They do not lose fur in the summer as most other mammals do. Their oily fur coat works very well. This means that all of the panda's heat stays inside its body and keeps it warm.

FUN FACT! Pandas swim across rivers to avoid predators or to find food.

Pandas live in areas where snow is common during colder months.

Keeping Safe

Pandas have few **predators** in the wild. Dholes are Asian wild dogs that sometimes kill young pandas for food. Leopards also sometimes attack pandas. Tigers were once a danger as well. These cats used to roam throughout panda **habitats**. But they have mostly disappeared from the places where pandas live and are no longer a threat.

Young pandas stay safe by climbing trees. They spend most of their time up high once they are old enough to climb. They can sleep and play in the trees, safe from predators.

Adults stay safe by scaring off or fighting attackers. They have sharp claws and sharp front teeth. They use these to swipe or bite at potential threats. Pandas' powerful jaws give them a dangerous bite. Pandas can also roar when they need to. This can scare off attackers.

Pandas can look fierce when they need to.

Mysterious Markings

Scientists are not entirely sure why pandas have their black-and-white markings. Some scientists believe that the markings can be used to intimidate other pandas. One panda might come too close to a second panda. The second panda can approach the first panda and stare it in the eyes. The black markings around the panda's eyes make the eyes seem bigger than they are. This could make the stare more intimidating and scare the other panda away. There is evidence to support this theory. An intimidated panda often covers its eyes with its paws. This could be so that it doesn't look as though the panda is trying to stare down an opponent.

Other scientists argue that the coloring is camouflage. The forests where pandas live are filled with shadows from trees and bamboo. A panda's black-and-white markings can help it blend in with the patterns of shadows on the ground.

Pandas cover their eyes to show that they don't want to fight.

CHAPTER 3

A Cub Is Born

Pandas usually only meet when it is time to **mate** and produce young. Mating happens each spring. A female panda begins marking objects with a special scent. Male pandas smell it and know that she is ready to mate. After mating season, the females go off by themselves again.

Female pandas give birth to cubs, or baby pandas, the following fall. A mother panda finds a hollow tree or a cave when it is time to give birth. This place is called a **den**. The den is a safe area for cubs to live in during the first months of their lives.

Cubs are born blind and helpless. They are also very small. Cubs are born weighing only a few ounces. A newborn panda is as small as a stick of butter. That means a panda mother is about 900 times larger than a cub.

Newborn pandas look a lot different than adult pandas.

A Cub's Life

A cub and its mother stay in the den for three or four months after it is born. The cub never leaves its mother during this time. The cub's mother holds it close during the first few weeks of its life. Sometimes the cub needs to change position to eat or sleep. The mother moves the cub around to make sure it is comfortable.

Like other mammals, female pandas produce milk to feed their young. The cub depends on its mother's milk until it is old enough to chew bamboo. Cubs grow very slowly. A cub is born with all-white fur. It takes about three weeks for its black-and-white markings to develop. It takes another month for the cub to be able to open its eyes.

FUN FACT! Pandas like to do somersaults.

Mother pandas are extremely protective of their cubs.

Growing Up

Cubs begin crawling when they are around 80 days old. At this time, a cub is able to move around on its own a little. But it is still not old enough to leave its mother's side. The cub can walk and run by the time it is three or four months old. Then it is finally time to take the first steps out of the den.

A cub takes its first bite of bamboo when it is just over a year old. It still drinks its mother's milk sometimes at this age. The cub slowly switches over to a full bamboo diet during the next year. This is called **weaning**.

Young pandas need to stay with their mothers for two winters. They are ready to leave their mothers when they are around two years old. Most settle down in an area close by. Others travel several miles away. The mother panda is ready to mate again after the cub leaves.

Young pandas need plenty of food while they are growing.

CHAPTER 4

All in the Family

Scientists have debated for years about which animals are most closely related to pandas. Many scientists believed for a long time that pandas were related to raccoons. The dark markings around the animals' eyes are similar. They also share some behaviors.

Other scientists argued that pandas were part of the bear family. Still others believed that pandas should be placed in their own category. Today, better technology has helped scientists look at pandas' DNA. This has helped them learn how pandas developed into the animals we know today. Most scientists now agree that pandas are related to bears.

Scientists also once believed that pandas were closely related to another bamboo-eating mammal. This other animal is often called a red panda or lesser panda. But red pandas are actually more closely related to raccoons than to pandas.

Scientists have learned about panda DNA from blood samples.

A Panda's Closest Relative

One of the panda's closest relatives is the spectacled bear. Like pandas, spectacled bears have dark patches of fur around their eyes. This makes them look like they are wearing glasses. They also share some other similarities with pandas. They live high up in mountain habitats and spend most of their time alone.

Spectacled bears live in the Andes Mountains of South America and other nearby mountain ranges. This is very far from where pandas live.

Unlike pandas, spectacled bears eat many different types of vegetation. This includes fruit and berries, cacti, and even tree bark. They also eat birds and small rodents.

Unfortunately, spectacled bears are in danger of going extinct. Farmers and poachers have killed many of them. Experts believe there are only about 3,000 spectacled bears remaining in the wild.

Spectacled bears and pandas have very similar faces.

CHAPTER 5

Protecting Pandas

Pandas once had a range that stretched across East Asia. They could be found in much of China. They lived as far north as the city of Beijing. And they lived farther south in today's countries of Myanmar and Vietnam. Some scientists believe that there was even a species of tropical panda. Their range started to shrink around 12,000 years ago. Tropical pandas went extinct. Today, pandas live only in a small stretch of mountains along the Tibetan Plateau. Small populations are scattered across about 5,000 square miles (13,000 sq km) of land.

Pandas today are endangered. This means that they are in danger of dying out completely. Scientists believe that there are only about 2,500 adult pandas in the wild today.

Pandas are treated with great respect when they enter towns or villages.

Harm from Humans

Humans are a large part of the problem. The human population grows rapidly every year. Humans need space to live and to grow food. As more humans are born, they need more space. Farms and villages in central China steadily move farther into the mountains. This often means taking over areas where pandas live. Herders often take their goats and other animals into panda habitats to find food.

Logging was a problem for a long time. Loggers cleared forests where pandas lived. This broke apart panda habitats. Small populations became isolated. Pandas could not always find new mates, and populations became less healthy. Young pandas did not have the space to make home ranges of their own.

Herders and their animals bother pandas when they travel into the mountains.

Disappearing Bamboo

Pandas sometimes struggle to find enough food. About once every 60 years, bamboo begins to grow flowers and seeds. The seeds fall to the ground and new bamboo plants begin to grow.

Pandas will not eat bamboo that has grown flowers. But it takes about 10 years for new bamboo plants to grow from the seeds of the old plants. This means pandas have very little to eat during these times.

The bamboo cycle runs on different schedules in different areas. In the 1980s, around 250 pandas starved to death during a bamboo shortage. Another shortage began in the mid-2000s. This shortage made it difficult for the National Zoo in Washington, D.C., to get enough bamboo to feed its pandas. Zookeepers kept the pandas from starving by getting permission to harvest bamboo from the property of local landowners.

The pandas at the National Zoo need plenty of bamboo to stay healthy.

Safe Homes for Pandas

Conservation organizations and governments are working to save pandas from extinction. China has created several **reserves** for pandas. Farmers and logging companies are not allowed to use land in these areas. Rangers who work at the reserves keep a lookout for poachers. These hunters kill pandas illegally. Poachers have played a large role in reducing panda populations.

Scientists are researching ways to increase the panda population. They look for ways to help pandas produce young in captivity. They hope to release these young pandas into the wild. Other scientists study how pandas interact with their environments. They track pandas that have been radio-tagged as they move through their home ranges. They hope to learn what pandas need from their habitats. They also learn about how pandas interact with the human population. This will help scientists figure out the best ways to protect pandas.

Scientists help pandas at China's Wolong Nature Reserve.

Zoos and Reserves

There are pandas living in zoos around the world today. But it is very hard to keep pandas healthy and happy in captivity. They often have trouble mating successfully in captivity. Cubs are rarely born. Today, most captive pandas live in China. The country often loans the pandas to zoos in other parts of the world. This gives people in other countries a chance to see pandas. Many people hope that this will raise awareness about protecting pandas.

It is also possible to visit pandas in China. Reserves often allow tourists inside the area. This brings in money to support the reserves.

Pandas are still in danger. Many scientists believe that panda populations are continuing to fall. But scientists, government officials, and other people around the world are working to protect the precious panda.

Zoos work to increase the world's panda population.

Words to Know

altitudes (AL-ti-toodz) — heights above ground or sea level

bamboo (bam-BOO) — a tropical plant with a hollow, woody stem

camouflage (KAM-o-flaj) — coloring or body shape that allows an animal to blend in with its surroundings

captivity (kap-TIV-i-tee) — the condition of being held or trapped by people

climates (KLYE-mitz) — the weather typical of a place over a long period of time

conservation (kon-sur-VAY-shun) — the act of protecting an environment and the living things in it

den (DEN) — the home of a wild animal

digest (dye-JEST) — to break down food in the organs of digestion so that it can be absorbed into the blood and used by the body

digit (DIJ-it) — a finger or toe

DNA (DEE EN AY) — the molecule that carries genes, found inside the nucleus of cells

endangered (en-DAYN-jurd) — at risk of becoming extinct, usually because of human activity

extinct (ik-STINGKT) — no longer found alive

family (FAM-uh-lee) — a group of living things that are related to each other

habitats (HAB-uh-tats) — the places where an animal or a plant is usually found herbivores (HUR-buh-vorz) — animals that only eat plants

home ranges (HOME RAYN-jiz) — areas of land in which animals spend most of their time

humid (HYOO-mid) — moist and usually very warm

intimidate (in-TIM-i-date) — to frighten someone, especially in order to make him or her do something

isolated (EYE-suh-lay-tid) — kept alone or separate

mammals (MAM-uhlz) — warm-blooded animals that have hair or fur and usually give birth to live young

mate (MAYT) — to join together to produce babies

molars (MOH-lurz) — wide, flat teeth at the back of the mouth used for crushing and chewing food

poachers (POH-churz) — people who hunt or fish illegally

predators (PREH-duh-turz) — animals that live by hunting other animals for food

reserves (ri-ZURVZ) — protected places where hunting is not allowed and where animals can live and breed safely

tropical (TRAH-pi-kuhl) — of or having to do with the hot, rainy area of the tropics

weaning (WEEN-ing) — gradually stopping the reliance on mother's milk for nourishment

PACIFIC

OCEAN

NORTH

AMERICA

ATLANTIC

SOUTH
AMERICA

Panda Range

Find Out More

Books

Firestone, Mary. *Top 50 Reasons to Care about Giant Pandas: Animals in Peril.* Berkeley Heights, NJ: Enslow, 2010.

Gallagher, Debbie. *Pandas.* New York: Marshall Cavendish Benchmark, 2010.

Greve, Tom. *Giant Pandas.* Vero Beach, FL: Rourke, 2011.

Web Sites

National Geographic Kids—Creature Features: Giant Pandas
http://kids.nationalgeographic.com/kids/animals/creaturefeature/panda
Visit this site to read facts, watch videos, and even listen to what a panda sounds like.

Smithsonian National Zoological Park—Giant Pandas
http://nationalzoo.si.edu/Animals/GiantPandas/PandasForKids/default.cfm
Look at tons of photos, play some games, and learn about what organizations are doing today to save the panda.

Visit this Scholastic web site for more information on pandas:
www.factsfornow.scholastic.com

Index

About the Author

Jennifer Zeiger earned a degree from DePaul University. She now lives in Chicago, Illinois, where she writes and edits books for kids.